Macmillan Caribbean

Trevor Rhone's fast-paced, laugh-out-loud comedies have an appeal that no other serious Caribbean playwright has been able to equal. *Bellas Gate Boy* is the most recent and one of the most successful of his works. A monologue, it revisits – through the playwright's own persona – Rhone's earliest experiences in live theatre. At the same time it explores the influences that eventually led him to the creation of a genuinely West Indian form of drama, earning him the title "father of Jamaican theatre". Rhone's enduring popularity reflects not only his gift for comic dialogue that sounds as natural as a conversation at a bus stop, nor his capture of essentially West Indian characters, settings and situations, but also his ability to use the laughter to spotlight for us social concerns that we need to address.

The Macmillan Caribbean Writers Series (MCW) is an exciting new library of fine writing which treats the broad range of the Caribbean experience. As well as plays, which include the Gayelle collections selected as particularly suitable for arts and drama festivals, MCW offers a wide choice of novels, novellas and short stories, by both new and established writers, and also embraces works of poetry and non-fiction. Writers on the list come from around the region, including Guyana, Trinidad, Tobago, Barbados, St Vincent, Bequia, Grenada, St Lucia, Dominica, Montserrat, Antigua, the Bahamas, Jamaica and Belize.

MCW was launched in 2003 at the Caribbean's premier literary event, the Calabash Festival in Jamaica. Macmillan Caribbean is also proud to be associated with the work of the Cropper Foundation in Trinidad, developing the talents of the region's most promising emerging writers, many of whom are contributors to MCW.

Judy Stone
Series Editor, Macmillan Caribbean Writers

Contents

Introduction	vi
Bellas Gate Boy	1
Act One	4
Act Two	22
Glossary	43

Introduction

The boy is father of the man. *Bellas Gate Boy* is the younger man's search for the boy's truth in order to find the path for the rest of his life.

Bellas Gate, birthplace of Trevor Rhone, is a tiny village on the border of the parishes of St Catherine and Clarendon on the Caribbean island of Jamaica. A special place of remembered innocence and simplicity, summoned up in the play to give evidence and inspiration but never to stand in judgement.

There is an old Jamaican saying, "If I don't laugh I'll cry", which echoes in the bones of most Jamaicans. This native philosophy often proves annoying and far beyond the understanding of others, especially when Jamaicans in the audience holler with laughter at the saddest bits. The sadder, the louder the laughter. Trevor Rhone has a sure-footed, instinctive cultural awareness in his work. In *Bellas Gate Boy* Rhone, master of comedy, is at his sophisticated best. He engages with horrendous instances of prejudice, racism, intolerance, inequality. By mixing them expertly with the yeast of the ridiculous, incidents which should, in the traditional way, be met with sympathetic but stern silence are effortlessly morphed into moments of high comedy, audience participation, and the genuine spontaneous laughter which comes from personal recognition.

Bellas Gate Boy explores the first thirty years of the playwright's life. It is written to be performed in two halves. However, the monologue consists of three distinct 'movements'. The first addresses his life in Jamaica from birth …

It is the year of our Lord nineteen hundred and forty. Jamaica is a British colony. King George the sixth sits on the throne of England. There is war in Europe. Bombs, guns going off. People are dying by the thousands. Thousands of miles away, at the Victoria Jubilee Hospital in Kingston, Jamaica, a baby boy is born. They name him, Trevor D Rhone.

… to the age of twenty-one. The second 'movement' examines his three-year period of study and survival in England at Rose Bruford College of Speech and Drama, 1961–4. The third sees him re-enter Jamaican society, and follows the difficult progress of relocation of self up until the Damascene moment which resulted in the writing of his first autobiographical work, *Old Story Time*, in 1979.

Rhone's mastery of the sounds and rhythms of Jamaican speech as he slips effortlessly from Standard English to the gentle patois of country folk, the harsh guttural urban rattle and the ultra refined uptown brown sound, is undisputed. It serves this piece well in performance as *Bellas Gate Boy* relies on swiftly recognisable characterisation, and agility – vocal, physical and mimetic – to keep the impetus. Precise dialects and accents are an essential, vital part of this feast of aural play. Every character has her or his own special tonality. Miss Mac's voice differs ever so slightly from Mrs Clarke's; the cadences in tone give away the class and circumstance of each player.

Of course to get the real music of the piece (which I think of as a tone poem), it needs to be heard. Keeping up the pace in the excerpt below is a test of breath control, vivid imagination and mastery of the rhythmic dialectic as it 'licks and jigs to the rhythm of the music'.

After (Christmas) lunch – dressed in new knickerbocker pants an' long socks, you crepe hat on you head, your tin fifi in your mouth an' you money in your pocket – it was down the road to join in the festivities. Merry Chrismus. The worl' an' his wife were there – Merry Chrismus – and me in the middle of it, buying grater cake, an' drops an' gizzada an' paradise plums an' mint ball, an' ice cream ... a sucking an' a licking an' a jiggin' to de riddim of the music coming from the dance at Big Yard. An' later in the day, goat race, horse race – the whole human race keeping pace with the fun.

Rhone's early years were comfortable and comforting, with the support of the whole community. The joy is infectious and wholesome.

I grew up with my family in Bellas Gate, in a big old ramshackle house. Deep rural. Mountainous. Mist-covered after the rain. Beautiful. Isolated. No radios. No telephones. Life was sweet. Life was harsh.

This was a useful grounding for the harsh realities which were to beset him when he left the familiar bosom of Jamaica. It is this grounding which permits him the grace to resist bitterness when he is greeted by "Keep Britain White" and "Niggers Go Home" slogans. He invites us to laugh with him at man's inhumanity to man.

Upon arrival, stranded at a London station with his cardboard suitcase, he asks a man how to get to Sidcup ...

- *You Jamaican?*
- *Yes ...*
- *Stone the crows. I was at Up Park Camp for a couple of years. Cor, dem beauties! Never forget Joyce. You don't know Joyce do you? Oh, Sidcup. Take the choob to Charing Cross and it's the loop line to Dartford, mate.*

Bellas Gate Boy is an important addition to the body of work from Caribbean writers who have explored the consequences and emotions of being uprooted from home. Claude McKay, writing from London in the 1920s, admitted:

I have forgotten much, but still remember
The poinsettia's red, blood-red, in warm December.[1]

In 1967, Cambridge-educated Kamau Brathwaite wrote:

Never seen
a man
travel more
seen more
lands
than this poor
path-
less harbour-
less spade[2]

It's probably safe to suggest that neither of the above has had them rolling in the aisles. Trevor Rhone on the other hand, on his first day at drama school in England in 1961, announces to all and sundry:

I am black as you can see, but I must warn you I do not sing, I do not dance nor do I play the drums.

---

[1] 'Flameheart' by Claude McKay, *Harlem Shadows*, Harcourt, New York, 1922.
[2] 'Rights of Passage' by Kamau Brathwaite, *The New Arrivants: A New World Trilogy*, Oxford University Press, Oxford, 1981.

He was of course in deadly earnest. A serious pronouncement meant to save him from future embarrassment, this pronouncement simply brought the house down. He really cannot sing, he cannot dance and would never be allowed to beat a drum in Jamaica as his rhythmic sense is so very, shall we say, individualistic. Somehow, however, he manages to find a comedic rhythm in his dialogue which almost never fails. Neither does it fail to deliver the political point, however harsh. Compare his Jamaican Christmas quoted earlier with his first Christmas in England:

The Christmas Eve party has been a dismal failure so the friends leave ...

> *New to England, we never know all public transport stopped running early on Christmas Eve. Taxi? Seven black men, after midnight? Try you bes'. We start walking. It is freezing. We walking, cussing. Cussing this godforsaken place.*

As soon as we, the audience, are about to settle back for a tirade about racist taxi drivers in the UK the spell is broken by:

First Christmas day in the UK when somebody shout,
– It a snow to blurd naught!
– You lie.
It snowed and snowed. We stoned each other with snow balls. Splatt. A white Christmas. I made me a snow woman and we danced, and danced, and danced, and she melted in my arms.

"Ahhhhh!" goes the audience. This sequence provides a terrific opportunity to make a series of telling political points without shouting, for the skilled actor to excel in a series of mimes and for the audience to experience the magic moment when the snow falls a long way from home. Yet a silent acknowledgement that behind the sentiment there is an iron fist in the calico glove is never far from the mind.

The new Trevor Rhone, fully qualified actor, having translated possible failure into success by invoking the Mohammed Ali (then Cassius Clay) call sign, 'I am the Greatest', returns home to Jamaica, with a perfectly produced voice embellished with an even more perfectly aristocratic English accent, punctuated by a rolled umbrella, and startles poor Miss Mac when, in answer to her enquiry after her son's health, she is informed he is:

Frightfully, frightfully good, thanks.

The new Trevor had forgotten the maxim entrusted to him by Edric Connor who, while encouraging him to attend Rose Bruford, had warned:

– Whatever they teach you – forget half of it.

He had instead, swallowed it hook, line and sinker. Serious mistake.

Bellas Gate Boy's dénouement, if on occasion a trifle sentimental, is dedicated to the recovery of his early appreciation of the importance of the mountain mists of his childhood, the time before 'Frightfully, frightfully good, thanks' was part of his vocabulary. His mother, Miss Mac, becomes the metaphor for the importance of working towards becoming a prophet in his own land.

Yvonne Brewster

Bellas Gate Boy

*A monologue
adapted for the stage by
Yvonne Brewster*

Characters

TREVOR
Others
[All characters are played by the same actor]

Bellas Gate Boy was first staged at the Barn Theatre, Kingston, Jamaica on 31st December 2002. The actor was Trevor Rhone, director Yvonne Brewster, set and costume design by Ellen Cairns.

Bellas Gate Boy

Set: The stage is a black box. Up centre, about four feet from the back of the set, is a free-standing flat which is also painted black, for entrances and exits. Suspended by invisible threads above the stage, torn ancient pages from the Psalms of David flutter. Downstage right and upstage left are huge piles of larger than life prop books sculpted from polystyrene foam and painted to resemble ancient tomes. These are used by the actor to create the world of the play. Above centre stage a snow bag is secreted.

There are few props: a blackboard which doubles as a tabletop, a suitcase, a Bible, an umbrella, an old reel-to-reel tape-recorder, some playscripts and a variety of hats used to indicate character.

Act One

TREVOR: It is the year of our Lord nineteen hundred and forty. Jamaica is a British colony. King George the sixth sits on the throne of England. There is war in Europe. Bombs, guns going off. People are dying by the thousands. Thousands of miles away, at the Victoria Jubilee Hospital in Kingston, Jamaica, a baby boy is born. They name him, Trevor D Rhone.

- *What's the D for?*
- *DEAR. His mother took one look at him and said, "What a dear!"*

I was that child. The twenty-third child of my father, Hezekiah Nathaniel Rhone – Mass Heze – and the third child of my mother, Rosamond Wilhelmina – Miss Mac. She was McCalla before marriage. I named her Mac … Aroni.

Miss Mac was a short, rather plump black woman. A school teacher. She'd started teaching at fifteen, at five shillings a month, yet Miss Mac would tell us:

- *Saved something out of it every month.*

Miss Mac was very frugal. She once said to me:

- *You know, Trev, if I had to live my life all over again, is one thing I would like to be.*
- *Whar's that Miss Mac?*
- *More frugal, Trev. More frugal.*

Yet she was always adopting some needy child. I remember once she brought this sickly-looking little boy home to live with us. You could hear Mass Heze:

– *Woman bring anodder pickney into the house. I am fed up!*

Mass Heze was an enormous brown man. His father came with a group of Haitians to prospect for gold in the hills of Bellas Gate. The mines failed and they all became cultivators working steep hillside lands that produced bananas, cocoa, coffee and pimento, for the export market.

I grew up with my family in Bellas Gate, in a big old ramshackle house. Deep rural. Mountainous. Mist-covered after the rain. Beautiful. Isolated. No radios. No telephones. Life was sweet. Life was harsh.

I spent my childhood playing and eating. Moving between my home and a sister who lived down the road, I would average six meals a day, with tons of fruit in between. I became quite round and they nicknamed me Tubby. I never got sick. The nearest doctor was ten miles away, by foot.

My greatest fear was the fear of the black-heart man who, it was rumoured, preyed on little children, cut out their hearts to work obeah. I was on an errand for Miss Mac one day when, in the distance, I heard the sound of a vehicle approaching. It didn't sound like the bread van, the only vehicle that came through once a week. I started breathing hard. Black-heart man? Oh God! My heart is beating faster now – beating through my shirt. I bolt through the bushes. I am moving now with the speed of light. My whole body is fluttering like a chicken that has lost its head. I run to safety in a neighbour's yard. I collapse from sheer fright.

I had an early awareness of sex. The animals were doing it. My brothers were doing it in the bushes. My father, I worked out, did it at least twenty-three times. I too at an early age wanted to do it. At six.

In Bellas Gate you didn't need a calendar to know when Christmas was coming. That ole Christmas breeze coming over the hill, right on time, was the cue for Christmas preparations to move into full gear. Sister Ivy's carollers, despite the cold, were out at 5 a.m. Joy to the world floated through the morning mist as I lay in my parents' warm bed.

That was comforting, but what you desperately needed for 'Chrismus' was money in yuh pocket, and not a penny to get from parents, which meant we had to be creative. Rat cut coffee. When the rats ate the ripe coffee berries, the beans would drop on the ground. I can still see myself on all fours searching for the rat cut coffee. I could so easily have raided the trees, but never did. Honour, trust, self-sufficiency, industry – lessons well learnt that have served me all my life.

Come Christmas Eve and time to sell the coffee. So, with money in my pocket, new clothes, the house painted, new curtains, new bedspreads, fence posts, tree trunks, walkway stones whitewashed, it was left for Mass Heze to kill the cow. What meat wasn't eaten over Christmas would be smoked and salted. We had beef for months.

Christmas morning breakfast was liver and kidney and light with hard dough bread and Johnny cakes and boil bananas, with steaming chocolate tea with the fat on top. And then for lunch, roast beef, with rice and peas and fried plantain, and vegetables. For dessert, Christmas cake and sorrel; but we could not eat until we took food for the shut-ins and the indigent in the district.

After lunch – dressed in new knickerbocker pants an' long socks, you crepe hat on you head, your tin fifi in your mouth an' you money in your pocket – it was down the road to join in the festivities. Merry Chrismus. The worl' an' his wife were there – Merry Chrismus – and me in the middle of it, buying grater cake, an' drops an' gizzada an' paradise plums an' mint ball, an' ice cream ... a sucking an' a licking an' a jiggin' to de riddim of the music coming from the dance at Big Yard. An' later in the day, goat race, horse race – the whole human race keeping pace with the fun.

I was six when Mass Heze took me to a Tea Meeting. Members of the community sang, recited, danced, told jokes, and made music. Ever' so often someone shouted:

– *Sixpence to take him down.*
– *Shilling to put him back.*

I thinking you take off or put back a man 'coz yuh liked or didn't like the performance. Come Mass Heze's turn. I was nervous for him ... Mass Heze did me proud.

– *The boy stood on the burning deck*
With a necktie tie round him neck.
Fire. Fire everywhere, burning through the midnight air
All is fair in love and war
Twinkle twinkle little star
How I wonder where you are
Oh Lochinvar. Oh Lochinvar.

A voice shouted:

– *Shilling to take him down!*

I got so vex. Mass Heze was the best performer. No idea that the event was to raise funds for the school. I had a farthing in my pocket. I shouted:

– *Farthing to put him back!*

Everybody laughed, but it was enough to put him back.

That night was the first time I saw live theatre. I knew then exactly how I would spend my days. Singing an' dancing an' reciting an' making music:

– *I am going to be so good, nobody will ever pay to take me off.*

I practised on the comb and paper, and the bamboo fife, even tried Miss Mac's organ – try as I might I couldn't turn a tune; like mother, like son. I gave up the music in frustration. My future reduced to singing an' dancing an' reciting. An' recite I did.

– *Old Zip Coon*
  There was once a man who could execute
  Old Zip Coon on a yellow flute
  And plenty of other tunes to boot
  But he couldn't make a penny
  with his tootle ti toot
  Tootle ootle ootle. Tootle ti toot.

  He met a singular quaint old man with a big tuba
  Who said he'd travelled near and far
  But he couldn't make a penny with his Umpa pa
  Umpa umpa umpa pa.

  They met with a man who was travelling
  With a big bass drum and a cymbal thing
  Who said he'd banged since early spring
  But he couldn't make a penny with his boom zing zing
  Boom zing. Boom zing. Boom zing zing.

  So the man with the flute played tootle ti toot
  And the other man he played umpa

And the man with the drum and the cymbal thing
Played Boom zing. Boom zing. Boom zing zing.

And oh the pennies that the people fling
When they hear the tootle ootle umpa Boom zing zing
Tootle ootle umpa. A Boom a zing a Boom a zing
Tootle ootle umpa Boom zing zing
Tootle ootle umpa a Boom a zing a Boom a zing
A tootle a tootle umpa zing.

Bartons Primary was rehearsing a song for the visit of the school inspector. I was singing at the top of my voice, when the teacher called me out and said:

– *Trevor. Don't sing.*

I thought she had a solo for me. Well, the inspection came and went. No solo. My aunt explained:

– *Trevor, God in his wisdom has not blessed you with a talent for singing.*

Okay, well then. I would dance. And recite.

I am twelve. It is 3 a.m. and I am saying goodbye to Mass Heze. I am leaving for Beckford & Smith's High School in Spanish Town on a scholarship.

– *Mass Heze, have anything to give Trevor?*

Miss Mac asked. There was a long pause, then Mass Heze turned and faced the wall, giving me his back. Mass Heze provided food and shelter. Miss Mac provided everything else. Goodbye, Miss Mac.

My first school fete. My first slow dance. I discovered my body was very sensitive. I kept pulling back. Was embarrassing, so, I danced to the faster beat. Soon I was getting a polite:

– *No thank you*

to my:

– *May I have this dance?*

Later, I overheard two girls:

– *That boy Rhone. He can't dance.*
– *No. He have two left foot.*

Left only with the talent to recite.
My school entered the school's drama festival and needed a small boy to play the back end of a donkey. I volunteered.

– *Get out!*

said the drama teacher who also taught maths:

– *You do no maths in my class, get out!*

The following year I tried harder at maths, and got into the drama club. The Drama Festival was at the Ward Theatre. The day I stepped into the Ward for the first time I entered an amazing and wonderful new world. We presented scenes from *Julius Caesar*. Poor Brutus, Cassius, Anthony, never stood a chance against an electrifying display of coarse acting by the First Citizen.

— *We'll burn the house of Brutus. Come away.*
  We'll burn his body in the holy place
  And with the brands fire the traitor's house.
  Take up the body.

As a proud possessor of a Drama Festival Award I moved to Kingston to pursue my passion.

In the newspapers, "AUDITIONS. Singers. Actors. Dancers. Needed for annual pantomime." I met Louise Bennett and Ranny Williams that day. Me and the stars in the same room! I avoided the singing and the dancing and knocked 'em dead with:

— *Friends, Romans, Countrymen. Lend me your ears.*
  I come to bury Caesar not to praise him.
  The evil that men do lives after them;
  The good is oft interred with their bones;
  So let it be with Caesar.

The producers thanked us:

— *It was ver' very good of you all to come to the Ward this morning. The Pantomime needs young blood. You will be hearing from us ver' very soon.*

A week, and no word from them. I met someone from the auditions.

— *Oh yes, me dear. I've heard from them. In fact I'm heading down the Ward right now. Rehearsals, you know.*

Rehearsals started. Without me? Nah, sah! I took myself down there. I sat in the auditorium and watched the rehearsals. I was back for the next rehearsal, and the next. People began to recognise me:

– *Hi. Hi. I am Trevor.*

The next rehearsal I made my move. I crept round the side and slipped onto the stage and joined the chorus. That rehearsal ended and nobody said anything to me. And they never did for three pantomimes in a row.

At eighteen I met Edric Connor, the great Trinidadian actor. I told him I was applying to Drama schools. He recommended the Rose Bruford College in the UK, with a caution:

– *Whatever they teach you – forget half of it.*

A letter came from the Rose Bruford. A Miss Yvonne Clarke, a Jamaican and recent graduate of the college, would give me an audition. I arrived exactly on time. She lived on a huge property that now houses the Barn Theatre.

– *Hello.*
– *Hi.*

Then I did my pieces, right there on her veranda. *Friends*. And then a more lyrical piece.

– *Whose woods these are I think I know*
  His house is in the village though;
  He will not see me stopping here
  To watch his woods fill up with snow

  The woods are lovely, dark and deep
  But I have promises to keep,

> *And miles to go before I sleep,*
> *And miles to go before I sleep.*[1]

No comments from her – just a polite

– *Thank you,*

and I was ushered out.

Few weeks later, news came – I'd been accepted. Major problem. To tell Miss Mac. She had her own visions for me. Teacher. Lawyer. Parson. I showed her the acceptance letter. She took me to see the priest. Didn't help, so a family meeting was called. My brother Neville was the most vocal.

> – *On no account, Miss Mac, spend any of your good money to send that damn idiot to go to study foolishness in England.*

I have a hundred pounds saved. With or without family help I am going to Drama School. I book my ticket, an' start to pack me suitcase.

Miss Mac hears about all this.

> – *Trev, I've brought you three pairs of pyjamas and this pair of long johns. Nice flannel. You goin' need a hat and a hymn book. If you really goin' I promise to help you with the money on one condition. You don't get into any trouble.*

I clutched that brown felt hat. I promised. I knew she had no understanding of this thing I was going to study. To be truthful, neither did I.

---

[1] 'Stopping by Woods on a Snowy Evening' by Robert Frost, *The Poetry of Robert Frost*, Henry Holt and Company, New York.

Departure day: Miss Mac and Aunt Syl were there to see me off. Miss Mac broke her promise and cried. The ship's horn sounded and the boat very slowly drifted away from my family and the shores of Jamaica.

Twenty-one days later, after a wretched time at sea, I arrived at Paddington Station. The college had written that I'd be lodging with a Miss Hammond who'd meet me on my arrival, which I had confirmed in a letter. All the others from the boat were soon gone. I was the only black face at the station. I'd be easy to find. An hour later I was still waiting. I had Miss Hammond paged.

- *Trevor Rhone, from Jamaica, is waiting by the information desk.*

Another hour goes by. No Miss Hammond. Maybe she didn't get my letter. I had her address, so I approached a passer-by and asked directions to Sidcup.

- *You Jamaican?*
- *Yes ...*
- *Stone the crows. I was at Up Park Camp for a couple of years. Cor, dem beauties! Never forget Joyce. You don't know Joyce do you? Oh, Sidcup. Take the choob to Charing Cross and it's the loop line to Dartford, mate.*

He was off before I could ask where I find the choob. So, I asked a bowler-hatted, pinstripe-suited, brolly-toting gentle-man.

- *Excuse me Sir. Sir. Where I find the choob?*
- *I suspect you mean the tube, don't you? Follow the signs.*

Keep Britain White. Niggers Go Home.

Exhausted and extremely hungry, I took a taxi from Sidcup station to Miss Hammond's address to find the house in darkness. I rang the doorbell repeatedly. No answer. I sense a policeman.

- *Hello. Hello. Hello there. As far as I know Miss Hammond is away on holiday.*

She was. For a week. I am up a creek. But God is good and angels abound. The neighbours invited me into their house. I write to Miss Mac. Her letter was wet with her tears, that I had received such kindness from strangers.

Miss Hammond returns.

I was one of three blacks in a student body of two hundred. On the first day the first years introduced themselves to the rest of the college. I was nervous as I stood facing a sea of white faces, and then in my best voice,

- *I am black as you can see, but I must warn you I do not sing, I do not dance, nor do I play the drums.*

In that very first week I was cast as the servant in the mime play, *L'Enfant Prodigue*. But, when I learnt the play was done to music I knew I had a problem. First rehearsal was a disaster. I stood, one left foot in front of the other left foot, waiting anxiously for the cue. It came and neither left foot would move ... I balanced backwards and forwards and sideways. Rose Bruford's face flooded with disbelief. After a couple of times of,

- *Let's try it again,*

Miss Bruford was heard to say,

- *He will not do.*

I was voted least likely to succeed.

My first Verse Speaking class. Finally a chance to redeem myself.

- *"Thistledown" by Andrew Young.*
  Hosts of bright thistledown
  Begin their dazzling journey through
  The air ...
- *STOP! Thistledown is light and fluffy. It floats in the air. You make it thud to earth like a boulder. Use the voice to paint a picture of this light fluffy thing floating through the air. Your speech is inarticulate, and as to your phrasing ... Oh! Hear it again next week.*

Weeks later I was still struggling with "Thistledown", while the others in my group had moved on to their fourth poem. I was falling behind and failing miserably at everything.

Voices from Jamaica came back to haunt me.

- *Miss Mac, on no account should you spend your good money sending that damn fool to England to study foolishness. Nah, sah! He can't sing. He can't dance.*

The voices around were not helping either.

- *Pater has gold mines in South Africa.*

Poor me. Depending on Miss Mac for next month's lodgings and pocket money, I was living off nine shillings a week. I was so poor I would buy a box of matches and cut each stick in four so I could get four strikes.

One Saturday in late November, it turned cold. I had to go up to London. Perfect day to wear my flannel long johns. On the train I had a compartment all to myself. I was enjoying the aloneness, when I felt the first itch. The train was heated. The long johns were on fire – Jesus Christ Rastafari! I had to get off the train. Phew! The cold air brought immediate relief. Thank you, Miss Mac, but never again.

I spent that first Christmas with Frank, a friend of mine from Jamaica. We came up on the boat together. Frank had a room in a rooming house in London. One bed in the room. I wasn't comfortable with the situation at all, but was so happy to escape Sidcup I decided to bunk it.

Eight days by Frank, I haven't had a bath. Why? I can't find the bathroom.

- *Frank. I need to bathe man. Whey the bathroom?*
- *Bring a towel an' come.*

I didn't question, I just followed in silence. After a long bus ride we join a queue. Frank goes in. I am next. I can still see the stains on that bath. I had to bathe. After all, it was Christmas Eve. We head home in silence.

We met up with Charlie Hyatt, Karl Binger and Vernon Estick that evening. What happening sah etc. We invited to a party that night. Promise of girls. We get to the party. Not a woman in sight. There were at least twenty men plus our seven.

- *Relax, Rhone. Woman coming.*

An hour later, more man arrive, and yet more man.

- *What the ... is this? No sah. This don't make no sense. Leaving this place, man. Come.*

New to England, we never know all public transport stopped running early on Christmas Eve. Taxi? Seven black men, after midnight? Try you bes'. We start walking. It is freezing. We walking, cussing. Cussing this godforsaken place.

- *Three mile.*
- *Dass all?*

We walking.

- *Time is it?*
- *What the ... you want know de time for? What difference it make?*

Ten mile. *(Nose starts streaming)*

- *Anybody have a tissue?*

London Bridge. And many more miles to go before I sleep.
(Snow starts to fall)
First Christmas day in the UK when somebody shout,

- *It a snow to blurd naught!*
- *You lie.*

It snowed and snowed. We stoned each other with snow balls. Splatt. A white Christmas. I made me a snow woman and we danced, and danced, and danced, and she melted in my arms.

My first year ended as it began, with me failing everything. There were fifty-five students in my year and I was fifty-fifth. Four students were asked to leave. I wasn't, I suspect for one of the following reasons:

- *He has come from far away.*
- *He pays his fees on time.*

- *Perhaps in time he will learn something to take back to his people.*

Holidays coming up. Got to earn some money, but I got that under control. A nursing sister at the hospital promised me a holiday job, so the first day of the holidays I was knocking on her door.

- *When is she coming back then?*
- *I see.*
- *Did she leave word about a job for Trevor Rhone?*
- *She made a firm promise ...*

I will do anything. Anything. Please. I am desperate. Thank you. I finally got the job. I made beds non-stop – patients calling me "Darkie". Nurses calling,

- *Come remove the bed pans, Darkie.*
- *DARKIE, dead man over here.*

Folks: the first time I had to wrap a dead man an' cart him out of the ward – folks, that night I was back in Bellas Gate – white duppies coming out of the wall.

My second year mirrored the first. We were down to fifty-one students in my year and I was fifty-first. I am convinced I would not graduate.

Beginning of my third year I am at my lowest ebb. It was do or die. Death of a dream.

Over the airways I hear a voice:

- *I am the greatest!*
  I am the greatest!
  This is the legend of Cassius Clay, the most beautiful fighter in the world today.

First time I heard a black person say, "I am black and I am beautiful." Soon after I had the confidence and the courage to write on the blackboard in the tiniest print, *I am the greatest, Trevor D Rhone*. After two years of being cowed and awed, the first signs of a new me were peeking out like crocuses in spring.

BBC Radio at that time sponsored a competition for final-year drama students. I volunteered. Nobody gave me a chance. To everybody's surprise, Trevor D Rhone makes the team. The BBC commended me. *I am the greatest!* I am saying it louder now.

My confidence is taking flight.

I challenge my two fencing instructors. A father and son team. They were both Olympic gold medallists. On guard. Parry. Riposte. Thrust. The daddy beat me, but I whupped the son.

My confidence is soaring.

I am asked to help first-year students with their voice and speech. My confidence is in orbit. *I am the greatest!*

Then, the college introduces Revue Techniques. Singing. Dancing. End of the class comes homework.

- *Each person is to bring for next week a music sheet. I want to hear you sing, individually.*
- *Sir. Can't sing, Sir.*
- *Nonsense.*

The following week I am back with a music sheet of "Day Oh. Day dah light an' mi wan' go home". The teacher picks on me first. The class breaks up into hoots of laughter. He plays the introduction. I let out:

- *Day Oh!*

The teacher looks at me as if he had seen his father's ghost.

- *Sit.*

I put that behind me and started preparing for the most crucial Verse Speaking recital of that third year.

RECITAL DAY.

The members of my year fell like ninepins that day. Come my turn, I approached the spotlight, took twenty seconds to prepare myself and started.

– *Sonnet 116 by William Shakespeare*
 Let me not to the marriage of true minds
 Admit impediment. Love is not love
 Which alters when it alteration finds,
 Or bends with the remover to remove;
 O no; it is an ever fixed mark,
 That looks on tempests, and is never shaken;
 It is the star to every wandering bark,
 Whose worth unknown, although his height be taken.
 Love's not Time's fool, though rosy lips and cheeks
 Within his bending sickle's compass come,
 Love alters not with his brief hours and weeks,
 But bears it out even to the edge of doom.
 If this be error, and against me prov'd,
 I never writ, nor no man ever lov'd.

The adjudicator took to the stage.

– *Never before in the history of English poetry have so many poets been brutally murdered in one place as happened here today. Thank God for Trevor Rhone who was like a beacon of light on this dark, dank day.*

My problems I thought were at an end. But trouble never sets like rain.

End of Act One

Act Two

TREVOR: Every year the College staged a major production. It was the most important calendar event for the College, usually staged at a big London theatre. Whatever the show I'd get a token part. So, I am cool.

- *It's been decided that the big show for this year will be* Green Pastures.

Green Pastures? Isn't that the play set in the deep south of America where the black people imagine they go to a black heaven? There is not a single white character in that play. Black angels. Black Moses. Black God.

- *Trevor Rhone to play God. The lead.* God!

What!!! From the shop piazza in Bellas Gate to the London stage in fifteen years. Too much, too soon.
The student body was up in arms. The entire cast except three would have to black up. Some from head to toe.

- *This woman and this black play for this ... nigger!*

I understood their anger. It was their chance to be seen in London, and who is going to see them behind a mask of black?
Janet Lees Pryce, the white Kenyan, is going home to see a witch doctor to do me in. I didn't take it on. I started reading the play and knew immediately I was in deep trouble.

- *(God enters)*
  God: Have you been redeemed?
  (Sings)
  God: Have you been baptised?
  (Sings)

Miss Bruford could not have forgotten the report from the Revue teacher.

- *Rhone can't sing. Can't dance.*

I learn a couple of pages, then I remember – *He sings* – and I forget everything. Janet Lees Pryce, the white Kenyan, has a black doll and is sticking needles in its throat. I didn't take that on either. It's a ten-week rehearsal. The worst ten weeks of my life. Secretly prayed that Miss Bruford would take me out of my misery. Every member of staff tried to help me. Couple of times we did the beginning I spoke the line,

- *You been redeemed …*
- *You have to sing it, Trevor.*
- *I know. I know. I am working on it.*

People in my year are waiting. Watching.

I am preparing for the dress rehearsal in London, and I get this funny feeling in my throat. I tried to cough. *(Cough.)* It hurts. Bad.

By the time I got to London that Friday evening I am totally sick. I cannot speak. I cannot swallow. I am running a high fever. That night the pain was so excruciating I did not sleep.

Saturday I am worse. I deteriorate further on Sunday. I have not eaten for three days.

Monday morning I drag myself to the theatre. Word gets to Miss Bruford that I am sick.

- *Psychosomatic,*

she says.

- *Tell that Trevor Rhone to get on the stage.*

I must have looked like death. She calls the doctor.

- *Rose. This is the worst throat I have seen in my forty years in medicine. Trevor has to go home immediately. I will write him a prescription. If there is no change in twenty-four hours, it's the hospital, I'm afraid. I am sorry.*

As I sat on the train to Sidcup, in pain, I was relieved. Knew I was bad in the part. As I lay in bed, I thought about Janet Lees Pryce pushing needles in the black doll's throat. My throat like knives going through it. Witch doctor? Black-heart man? My heart started beating fast. Beating through my shirt. I am back in Bellas Gate. Oh my God. The twenty-third Psalm. Just in case. Just in case. Just in case.

- *The Lord is my shepherd; I shall not want.*
  He makes me to lie down in green pastures ...

Green Pastures. Green Pastures.
Oh my God! The link! Cold sweat. Shivers all over my body.

- *He leadeth me beside the still waters*
  He restoreth my soul
  He guideth me in the paths of righteousness
  For his name's sake
  Though I walk through the valley of the shadow of death
  I will fear no evil for you are with me.

Then Psalm 1:

- *Blessed is the man that walketh not in the counsel of the ungodly*
  For the Lord knoweth the ways of the righteous
  But the ways of the ungodly shall perish.

And read through to Psalm 150:

- *Praise ye the Lord. Praise God in His sanctuary*
  Praise him with the timbrel and dance
  Praise him with stringed instruments and organs
  Let everything that hath breath
  Praise ye the Lord.
  King of Kings. Lord of Lords
  Mightiest in the mightiest.

I began to get an understanding of the power of God. For the first time I understand the character. All powerful. I had to get back to London for the nine o'clock rehearsal.

- *I've got to get better.*
  Though I walk through the valley of the shadow of death I will fear no evil – no evil.
  Though I walk through the valley.

I am scared to try my throat, but I must. A hoarse, gravelly sound. The first sound in days. I've got to get back to London. I've got to get back. Got to get back. Got to get back to London. The train is full. The litany goes on in my head to the rhythm of the train:

- *Though I walk through the valley …*

I can barely stand.

– *The Lord is my shepherd ... Hold my hand.*

I arrive at the theatre to see my understudy in my costume, putting on a black face. He sees me in the mirror.

– *Oh my God!*
– *I am here ...*

In a voice free of pain.
Word spreads like bush fire.

– *Trevor is here.*
– *Trevor is here.*
– *King of Kings. Lord of Lords.*
  Mightiest in the mightiest.

I waited in the wings. All the time in bed I had not once thought about the singing. All God's children were waiting.

– *Have you been redeemed?*
– *Yeah, Lord!*
– *Have you been baptised?*
– *Yeah, Lord!*

And as the spirit moved through me, one left foot disappeared and a right foot appeared, and I am moving like a breeze through the trees. Miss Bruford stopped the rehearsal.

– *Trevor? Trevor! I have never seen you so good. It's ... It's a MIRACLE!*
– *Have you been redeemed?*
  Yeah, Lord!

The show got rave reviews. Yvonne Clarke, from my audition in Kingston, came backstage to congratulate me.

– *Thank you, I have proved you right.*

Few days later, after the show closed, I was back in College.

– *Trevor, you got your diploma.*
– *Oh, really?*
– *And you got seven of the awards.*
– *Seven? I thought there were eight.*

Time to go home, but maybe after those rave reviews, maybe just maybe I could make it in London as an actor. There was little or no work for black actors, but I was special, so like all the wannabe actors in my year I started watching the post. Waiting for the phone to ring. It rang, but not for me. Letters came, but none for me. Everyone in my year got work, except me.

The realisation there was nothing here for me. Time to go home. Home to what? To Bellas Gate? Would be great to see Miss Mac. *(Reaches for suitcase, hat and umbrella.)* I arrived in Kingston with one Willie penny in my pocket.

Miss Mac cried tears of joy to see me. I greeted her rather coolly, in a sort of stiff-upper-lip British sort of way.

– *What's happening, Miss Mac? ...*
– *Frightfully, frightfully good, thanks.*

Then it dawned on me that the College had moulded me in their own image. I had not heeded Edric Connor's warning.

– *Whatever they teach you – forget half of it.*

I had swallowed it all, hook, line and sinker. I was a mimic man – British accent, tweed jacket and an umbrella. Of course I felt superior. Plenty people at the time thought I was a bit of a pappyshow. Didn't belong there. Didn't belong here either. I needed to undress and reclothe myself. But how?

Money? None. I had to find work. The Theatre in Jamaica was amateur. Shows played for three nights.

Got a job teaching school. Three days a week. Kingston College.

Miss Mac visited the school often to see if I was really there, teaching.

- *Teaching what?*
- *Drama, Miss Mac. Drama.*
- *They paying you?*
- *Yes, Miss Mac.*

As always she slipped a little money in my pocket, convinced I was not getting paid for teaching ... this "*Drama*".

Soon after, I got another two days at a school in a very depressed part of town. One of my duties was to take the attendance register. I soon discovered that the pregnancy drop-out rate was very high.

- *Virginette Smith ...*

A voice would pipe up.

- *Name and nature, Sir.*

A couple of weeks later:

- *Virginette Smith ...*
- *She not coming back, Sir.*

Who turns up one day? Yvonne Clarke ... -Jones. Hmm. Looking at the wedding band finger. Very nice.

She was home and looking for work, and soon enough we were sitting side by side in the staffroom at Kingston College.

Teaching was fine, but our hearts were in the Theatre. Six other theatre graduates returned home at about the same time, and we formed "Theatre 77". Objective? Professional theatre in Jamaica in twelve years. 65 to 77. We announced our first production with great fanfare and razzmatazz. Sydney, the man in charge, was a razzmatazz man.

I taught two jobs and then it was off to rehearsals. (*Collects old Grundig reel-to-reel tape-recorder, suitcase with props and costumes, a script and an umbrella.*)

– *Where is the damn bus? Come on.*

It was one bus, then another bus, and then ... it was at least a mile and a half walk to the theatre.

– *And many more miles to go before I sleep,*
   And many more miles ...

Our venue was the old dramatic theatre at the University,

– *Seating 1,500 souls.*

Dress rehearsal? Disaster. Opening night, everybody in the cast, especially Pat Priestly and Munair Zacca, nervous. Sydney arrives. Programmes. Programmes? I take a look at a programme. Makes a statement? It does. And the paper? Very nice. And the gold against the black? (*Gives Sydney the thumbs up sign.*)

– *How many you print, Sydney?*

- *Five thousand.*
- *Five?*
- *A thousand people per night. Ten-night run. A programme per couple.*
- *Okay.*

Showtime was eight o'clock. Ten to eight I peek out from backstage into the auditorium. Not a soul in the house. Eight o'clock. No change.

- *Hold for five,*

said Sydney.

- *I got scores of people coming. But you know Jamaicans. Always late. They'll be here.*

We ended up with four people that night. Three were complimentary. Complimentary programmes. Our total box-office take? Seventy-five cents.

There were two plays. The first play, Zoo Story. I was the man on the bench, reading a book. Very little to say. Sydney, the other character, was all around me with some long spiel about a dog. Running time of the play? About fifty minutes. Five minutes into the performance I realise we on the last page ... Panic ... Serious panic. Oh my God. What to do? I had to communicate with Sydney somehow. *(Various gestures.)*

- *(Sotto voce) Sydney. Sydney. Go back to page three. Page three, Sydney.*

Sydney like an on-rushing train kept rushing toward the end.

Two minutes later, the play done. *(Curtain call.)* Backstage, Sydney, all smiles.

– *Went really quickly tonight, didn't it?*

If I had a brick.

But the show must go on. I had to get dressed real fast for the next play, Miss Julie. I am playing Jean, the servant, trying to seduce Miss Julie. Yvonne. The lady of the house. We were outside at a party drinking and dancing up a storm. *(Dances and cavorts with her – very sexual.)*

We come on stage tipsy, and I reach for a bottle of wine. Got my eyes on her body. The wine bottle is an inch from my lips, when Yvonne hits the bottle away from my mouth. Completely out of character.

– *What?*

She points to the bottle – ugh! A roach swimming around in the wine. Sydney, God rest his soul, was stage manager in charge of props. Yvonne cuss him dat night. She cuss him. She cuss him.

After all the conflict and the drama of that very eventful opening night I picked up the old Grundig tape-recorder, the suitcase with props and costumes. I was at my lowest ebb. If ever I was to give up the theatre it was this night.

The show closed. Prematurely. All we had to show for our efforts were some very bruised egos, 4997 black and gold programmes and a mountain of debt.

I called a meeting.

– *We all met. Good. Sydney, I am demanding your resignation. Pen. Paper. Write it.*

A sotto voce female voice remarks,

- *Who does Mr Rhone think he is? Like he is still playing God.*
- *I don't have to put up with this.*
- *Then resign. Pen. Paper.*

And resign they did, till there were three of us left.
I looked at Yvonne and Munair in silence.

- *We start again?*

They nodded.

- *But first we got to pay off this mountain of debt.*

We did not know where to start. Who to turn to? But God is good and angels abound.
Yvonne's mother, Mrs Clarke, heard of our plight.

- *Bring me the books.*

She paid off our debts and was our benefactor for seven years.
To cut costs, we rehearsed our next production on Yvonne's veranda, right next to her father's bedroom, so we had to leave out all the swear words and be very, very quiet.

- *(Whispered) Phillipa. Phillipa. Where are you?*

One night, a message from Mr Clarke.

- *Go rehearse in the garage.*

(*Response to the command: whispered conversation with Yvonne, "Where the garage?" "Round the back"; pick up tape-recorder and other props and tiptoe off the veranda to the garage.*)

Freedom!

We pushed the cars out ... (*Mime pushing car out.*)

- (*Full voice*) *Phillipa. Phillipa. Where are you?*

... and back in after every rehearsal. (*Mime pushing car in.*)

- *'Von, if we cleared out all that junk, could put the play on here.*
- *Yeah.*
- *Ask your mum.*

Mrs Clarke bought into our madness, so we abandoned the rehearsals and set about cleaning out the garage. It took us weeks working round the clock, after school, weekends, to clear the mountain of junk. Finally we are done, except for this bath. Weighed a ton.

- *Come, Mr Drummond, come give us a hand with this bath.*

Mr Drummond was Mrs Clarke's eighty-year-old gardener. Mr Drummond came, took one look at the bath and said,

- *Move. Move.*

Single-handedly he grabbed it and got it out of there.

Amazing.

It was altogether an amazing time of our lives as we set about rehearsing an English farce, *How is the World Treating You?*, for the opening of the "Barn Theatre". Time to open the show. We had no money to buy or rent chairs. Quandary. 'Happening' was the buzz word at the time. We'd turn the opening into a Happening. 'Bring your own cushion.' Come opening night, the big question. Would anybody show up? 8.30 curtain. 8.15, nobody. Cars kept coming down the road. Coming down the road. Five people with cushions. My heart just kept on jumping out of my shirt.

- *Yes. Welcome to the Barn. That'll be two dollars and fifty cents. Enjoy the show.*

Thank you, Lord.

On a good night we took in twenty-five dollars at the box-office, and over the years every dime went to a new lighting board. A stage. One day, sixty sparkling new chairs arrived. I looked at Yvonne.

Present from her mother.

Mrs Clarke was our mentor and our threshold guardian, fierce in our defence, like the night she attacked this demon critic:

- *If you are here to give these children a bad report then leave now. Out. Out.*

The poor man quivered in his boots, stayed, and wrote us a glowing review. It was a good show, but there was nothing coming from the stage that mirrored the lives of the audience. And that became very important to us, except we had no plays. *(Looks at the umbrella with some disgust and discards it.)*

I was at the bus stop once, and I am hearing all these sounds.

All the sounds England had taught me to reject. Nice sounds, but underneath I could hear the pain, the hopelessness of a people who, like me, had lost their identity.

At home I took off the jacket for the last time *(mimes taking it off and dropping it beside the umbrella)*, and I wrote out the voices at the bus stop.

- *Wha' 'appen, bredda?*
- *Nutten.*
- *Wha' 'appen?*
- *Nutten nuh 'appen.*
- *No. Nutten nuh 'appen yet.*
- *You a hol' awn?*
- *Yes, I a hol' awn.*
- *Wha' you a hol' awn fah?*
- *Nutten. Jus' a hol' awn.*
- *A see.*
- *Ah A look two.*
- *Ah A look two too.*
- *Two tuff.*
- *Tuff.*
- *A want go dung ...*
- *Dung so?*
- *Yeah. Dung so.*
- *Whey you a go dung so fah?*
- *Nutten. Jus' a go dung.*
- *A see. I a hol' awn.*
- *Come nuh.*
- *Whey?*
- *Dung so.*
- *Wha' fah?*
- *Ah look two.*
- *Ah look two too.*

- *You see Spree?*
- *Spree?*
- *Spree.*
- *No. ... 'Ole awn.*
- *Wha'?*
- *Dem no ketch 'im?*
- *Wha' fah?*
- *Fe look two.*
- *When?*
- *Yessiday.*
- *Whey?*
- *Dung so.*
- *Rahtid. Whey 'im dey?*
- *'Im nuh dey deh.*
- *Whey?*
- *Up dey.*
- *Rahtid. Spree spree out.*
- *Spree spree.*
- *'Im was a look two.*
- *Ah look two too.*
- *Two tuff.*
- *Tuff.*
- *How long now you a look two?*
- *Ah A look two too long.*
- *Too long.*
- *'Ole awn.*
- *Angh ... Wha'?*
- *Whey Spree 'ooman?*
- *Which one?*
- *The last one.*
- *The last one? Aoh. Big Jill.*
- *Yeah. Big Jill.*
- *She a breed.*

- *Yeah.*
- *You feel a time gwine come fi get two?*
- *Long time.*
- *Too long.*
- *Wha' we gwine do?*
- *Ah don' know.*
- *You know what A wan' do?*
- *Wha'?*
- *A wan' do sompn.*
- *Wha' fah?*
- *Just fi do sompn.*
- *Like wha'?*
- *Like ... like ... like ...*
- *Like Spree?*
- *No. Nuh like Spree. Dem ketch Spree.*
- *You t'ink a time gwine come fi get two?*
- *Long time.*
- *Whey we going do?*
- *A don' know.*
- *Dem say ...*
- *Who dem?*
- *Dem dat always say.*
- *Oh, dem!*
- *A t'ink A gawn.*
- *Me nuh t'ink ... me gawn.*
- *You know ...*
- *Wha'?*
- *Nutten.*

I was running between two schools, two radio stations and the theatre. It was frantic, and was to get even more so after the headmaster at St Andrew Technical demanded I put on a Christmas pantomime with the students.

I spent the next two weeks scurrying around from one library to the next trying to find a script for the Christmas pantomime. *(He finds the scripts from the available pile of books.) Puss in Boots, Jack and the Beanstalk.* Read them to the children – they looked back at me with deadpan bored faces.

- *Sir, I can't find anything that interests the children. Have an idea what might, but it's not in the library, Sir.*
- *Where is it, then?*
- *Oh, it's in my head ...*
- *Oh well, then skip classes and write it down.*

A week later, I had a script. *Cinderella*, set in the children's environment. They read it and loved it.

A week into rehearsals, I walked into a crisis. Hundreds of black children and staff screaming at me.

- *How you could do a thing like dat, Missa Rhone – cast dat girl Janice as Cinderella?*
- *She too black.*
- *We want dat girl – de fairskin girl you cast as de fairy godmother.*
- *She 'ave to be Cinderella.*

My poor black traumatised Cinderella wanted out. *(Calls her over.)*

- *Janice.*

I consoled her.

- *You are black and you are beautiful, with the most beautiful voice and the best actress in this school. You are my Cinderella. No you, no show. So come on, let's rehearse.*

Yvonne came to help me, and helped restore Janice's confidence. Come opening night, Janice sang like a bird. Standing ovations. Janice didn't need the fairy godmother to turn her into a princess. She was. Now the centre of attention, courted by every boy in the school. Couple of months later I was taking the attendance register.

– *Janice Evans ... Janice ...*
– *She not coming back, Sir.*

My own life was on a treadmill. Round the clock, seven days a week. The stress is eating away at me, frustrations. Been thinking of trying my hand at writing a play, but no time to think. It came to a head in the staffroom at Kingston College. A year ago I had bought myself a Volkswagen – 150 dollars, way above my budget. The car had gone like a dream for months when some idiot said to me,

– *Rhone, when last you service your car?*
– *Service?*
– *Cars need servicing.*
– *Yeah, man.*

So, like an idiot, I get the car serviced. A week later it leaves me on the road. I needed to go check on it.

– *Borrow you car, Mr Brown?*
– *Sure, Mr Rhone, but little problem with the steering wheel. It tends to collapse.*
– *No problem.*

It collapsed. Piece in me right hand, piece in me left, piece fly on the dashboard, another piece roll gone under the seat.

Took me forty-five minutes to reassemble the wheel. I got out the car gingerly, and closed the door.

I sat in that staffroom and looked across at Mr Brown and I saw myself twenty-five years on, a frustrated old man with my life collapsing around me.

I turned to Yvonne.

– *This is my last day.*

I resigned with immediate effect. Health reasons. Felt good. Later that day I resigned the radio jobs. Felt even better. The car repair bill left me with no money for next month's rent. How you going manage, Rhone, on two days' teaching? By the sweat of thy brow. Come on, Rhone. Write. The rent? Couldn't focus on anything – except the rent. Lord help.

(The phone rings.) ... Hello ... *(listens.)* Ad agency want me for a commercial. Fifty dollars. *(Phone rings.)* ... Hello ... Same agency. Script problems. Got to reshoot. Another fifty. *(Phone rings.)* Them again. They'd like to apologise but there was a technical problem with the sound. No problem, I'll be happy to re-record. Where? Miami. Perfect. Another fifty plus expenses. Enough money to last me for six months. Thank you, Lord ...

Act One. Scene One. Page One. ... I know I want to write a play, but who for? Jamaica? Don't make no sense, Rhone. Play run for ten nights if you lucky. Can't live off that. Ahm. *(Quandary.)* London? New York? Plays run for months. Years. Yeah. London ... The pain ... Doors in my face. Name in lights ... weeks. Pulled. Tugged. Jamaica. London. London. Jamaica. Yes. Jamaica. Then self-doubt set in. Can't work, Rhone. Can't work. Waste a time. London.

Then, a tiny voice in my head. Bellas Gate. The place I escaped from. The joys of childhood. The first sounds. The foods. The smells. The things I never spoke about – buried deep inside me. My grandmother, who wouldn't have a black chicken in her yard. Miss Mac forever straightening my nose. Endlessly brushing my hair. Her choice of a woman for me to marry. The fairskinned Levine girl with the tall hair down her back. My resentment, anger at her. I had to get it out me system. Talk about it. Write about it, Rhone. Act One. Scene One. Page One. Trevor D Rhone, the first draft of what was to become *Old Story Time*. All the fervour and passion and repression in my soul poured out like an endless stream of lava and love.

– *Ah, Miss Mac. Miss Mac. To hug you, love you – free of all the conditioning in the world. Free at last. Free at last. Thank God. I am free at last!*

The End

Glossary

A	I (remains as 'I' when used for emphasis)
'coz	because
cuss	curse
dat	that
dem	them
dis	this
drop	small (often coconut) cake made of batter dropped on a baking sheet
duppy	ghost, apparition, evil spirit
gizzada	coconut tart
grater cake	coconut cake/sugar cake/chip chip cake
light	the lung of the animal
mi	my
nah sah	no sir
nutten	nothing
odder	other
paradise plum	hard sugar-coated boiled plum
pickney	child
riddim	rhythm
sah	sir
yuh	your (when used as an adjective: e.g. "yuh head")
	you (when used as a pronoun: e.g. "where yuh going?")

The Macmillan Caribbean Writers Series

edited by Judy Stone

Non-fiction:

… and the Sirens Still Wail: *Nancy Burke*

Novels:

Jeremiah, Devil of the Woods: *Martina Altmann*
Butler, Till the Final Bell: *Michael Anthony*
For Nothing At All: *Garfield Ellis*
Such as I Have: *Garfield Ellis*
Joseph – A Rasta Reggae Fable: *Barbara Makeeh Blake Hannah*
Walking: *Joanne Haynes*
The Boy from Willow Bend: *Joanne C Hillhouse*
Dancing Nude in the Moonlight: *Joanne C Hillhouse*
Alonso and the Drug Baron: *Evan Jones*
Ginger Lily: *Margaret Knight*
Exclusion Zone: *Graeme Knott*
Brother Man: *Roger Mais*
The Humming-Bird Tree: *Ian McDonald*
There's No Place Like … : *Tessa McWatt*
Trouble Tree : *John Hill Porter*
Ruler in Hiroona: *G C H Thomas*

Plays:

Bellas Gate Boy: *Trevor Rhone*
Two Can Play, with School's Out & The Power: *Trevor Rhone*
Champions of the Gayelle: *(ed. Judy Stone)*
  Plays by Alwin Bully, Zeno Constance & Pat Cumper
You Can Lead a Horse to Water: *(ed. Judy Stone)*
  Plays by Winston Saunders, Dennis Scott & Godfrey Sealy

Poetry

    Poems by Martin Carter: *(ed. Stewart Brown & Ian McDonald)*

Stories:

    Going Home and other tales from Guyana: *Deryck M Bernard*
    The Sisters and Manco's Stories: *Jan Carew*
    Chutney Power: *Willi Chen*
    The Fear of Stones: *Kei Miller*
    Popo and Stories of Corbeau Alley: *Nellie Payne*
    The Annihilation of Fish and other stories: *Anthony C Winkler*
    Under the Perfume Tree: *(ed. Judy Stone)*